KAKEBO

The Japanese Art of Saving Money

家計簿

INTRODUCTION

If, like many of us in Britain, you have never heard the term before, Ka-ke-bo is a combination of three Japanese characters (家計簿) which mean, literally, 'book of accounts for household economy'. That, in essence, is what this book is – and yet it offers so much more.

The Japanese are huge savers, and believe that financial stability is a key factor for wellbeing: tidy finances are as powerful as tidiness in one's house. Kakebo is central to that philosophy, an approach to spending and saving that also represents a pathway to balance and calm.

A Japanese tradition

The term 'Kakebo' was coined by Hani Motoko (1873-1957), a pioneer in almost every sense of the word. Born into a time of Japanese revolution and modernisation, she was the only girl in her school year, and one of the first generation of women to study at the Japan Women's University in Tokyo. She later became Japan's first female journalist and also founded Jiyu Gakuen Girls' School, unique for its educational ethos which advocated freedom, self-discovery and independence for women.

As a reporter, in 1903, Hani Motoko created *Katei No Tomo*, now the oldest women's magazine in circulation (its name changed to *Fujin No Tomo* in 1906, meaning 'the woman's companion'), in which she urged readers to undertake daily monitoring of their income and spending. In 1904, Hani Motoko published the first ever Kakebo – a household accounting book designed to help ordinary people bring order to their finances in a mindful way – which spread widely throughout society.

In the 1940s, Kakebo became so popular that the first Federation of Books for Household Savings was founded. These days there are millions of people both in Japan and across the globe who use their Kakebo every day to manage their spending and control every penny.

Now, with this English language edition, you can join them.

Make your Kakebo work for you

Using your Kakebo is easy. At the beginning of each month, you simply think about how much you would like to save and what you need to do to achieve your goal. You then jot down your weekly spending and at the end of the month tally everything up so you can see at a glance where your money is going.

This book offers 12 blank calendar months, so you can start at any point in the year. There are slots to personalise your Kakebo according to your own spending routine and lifestyle, and space to reflect and make changes as you go along. You'll also find graphs and questionnaires to help you see how things have progressed over the year.

Keeping a check on your daily bills requires a little discipline but it gets easier with practice. You will find that the simple act of using a pen and paper makes managing your accounts a healthy, mindful part of your everyday life.

"If we command our wealth,
we shall be rich and free. If our wealth
commands us, we are poor indeed."

EDMUND BURKE

HOW TO USE YOUR KAKEBO: STEP 1

At the beginning of each month, prepare the ground by noting down what you expect to have coming in (salary, other income, etc) and what you expect to go out as fixed expenses (utility bills, mortgage payments, etc). You can then decide what you have left for everyday spending (transport, food, going out, etc) and set yourself a savings target.

Detail your projected *income* – whether it be monthly salary, benefits or a gift.

If your income is not consistent each month (i.e. if you do temp or freelance work), make an educated guess.

[TIP: *round everything up to whole numbers to make calculations simpler.*

List your **regular outgoings** here. That's anything that recurs each month, such as utility bills, season tickets and credit card payments.

[TIP: *use previous bills for anything you need to estimate, and don't be afraid to round numbers up – it's better to plan for higher costs than lower.*

PLANNING THE MONTH AHEAD

Note down your projected income for the month:

INCOME (e.g. salary, freelance work, benefits, lodger...)		
Date	Source	Amount
15th	Salary	£1,950
1st	Lodger	£450
	TOTAL	£ 2,400

And list your regular expenses and outgoings:

REGULAR OUTGOINGS (e.g. rent/mortgage, utilities, phone, parking permit, gym membership, home/car/health insurance, credit cards/loans...)			
Bill / expense	Amount	Bill / expense	Amount
Mortgage	£900	Car	£150
Season ticket	£140	Council tax	£55
Mobile phone	£22	Water	£15
Gas/electric	£45	Home insurance	£35
Broadband	£20	Credit card	£127
		TOTAL	£ 1,509

FAQs:

1. What if my income is less than expected?
It is always best to underestimate your income and overestimate your costs; if you are uncertain about any potential payments coming in this month it's best not to include them in your projections.

2. What if a bill is more than expected?
If the difference is negligible, don't worry too much about it. If it turns out to be substantially more than expected, add it as an "Unexpected Extra" in the Weekly Diary when it comes in.

3. Not all of my expenses are monthly; some are charged annually. How do I account for this?
You can either include the entire amount in the expenses projection for the month in which the bill is due, or spread the cost as monthly payments in the period leading up to billing time.

MONTH: **February**

Work out how much you have to spend this month and decide what you want to save:

Total projected income:	£ 2,400
Less regular expenses:	£ 1,509
What's left for you to spend?	£ 891
How much do you want to save this month?	£ 300

Subtract your *regular outgoings* from your *income* to find out how much you are likely to have left to spend this month.

Set yourself a savings target.

What are your aims for this month?

- Put aside money towards holiday
- Spend less eating out

And how do you hope to achieve them?

- Take lunchbox to work every day

Make a note of any aims you have, short- or long-term.

HOW TO USE YOUR KAKEBO: STEP 2

Now that you have an idea of what you have available for the month and what you want to save, use these weekly charts to record your spending as you go. Your aim is to spend within your projected limits, and hopefully achieve your savings target. Your daily spending is split into four categories, ranging from essential living expenses to pleasure and entertainment. The Japanese believe that balance and variety is all – it's not just about the amount you spend, but how you spend it and why.

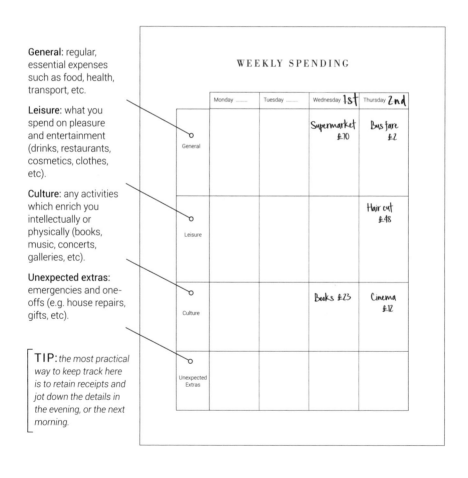

General: regular, essential expenses such as food, health, transport, etc.

Leisure: what you spend on pleasure and entertainment (drinks, restaurants, cosmetics, clothes, etc).

Culture: any activities which enrich you intellectually or physically (books, music, concerts, galleries, etc).

Unexpected extras: emergencies and one-offs (e.g. house repairs, gifts, etc).

TIP: *the most practical way to keep track here is to retain receipts and jot down the details in the evening, or the next morning.*

WEEKLY SPENDING

	Monday	Tuesday	Wednesday 1st	Thursday 2nd
General			Supermarket £70	Bus fare £2
Leisure				Hair cut £48
Culture			Books £23	Cinema £12
Unexpected Extras				

Each month is arranged as five weeks-to-view. The month names are blank, so you can start whenever you like, and the dates are blank so you can start recording from the first day of the month, whichever day of the week that happens to be (see the example below, where the 1st of the month falls on a Wednesday). In any cases where you end up with the odd day or two over at the end of the month, you can carry them forward and tuck them in at the beginning of the next one.

MONTH: **February**

	Friday 3rd	Saturday 4th	Sunday 5th	TOTAL
General	Food £15			£87
Leisure	Pub drinks £28	Meal out £38 Taxi £10		£124
Culture			Swimming £4	£39
Unexpected Extras	Flowers for Mum £15			£15

TIP: the category totals will be useful for your review of your monthly spending.

HOW TO USE YOUR KAKEBO: STEP 3

At the end of the month you can bring forward the totals from your weekly spending charts to review how things have gone.

Note down the weekly totals for each of the categories on your spending charts and add up the totals for the month.

TIP: *you can compare your spending and saving numbers month-on-month in the annual review pages at the back of the book.*

How did you do? Have you managed to stay on track and achieve the targets you set yourself?

Remember: the amount you actually had available to spend may well differ slightly from what you projected at the beginning of the month.

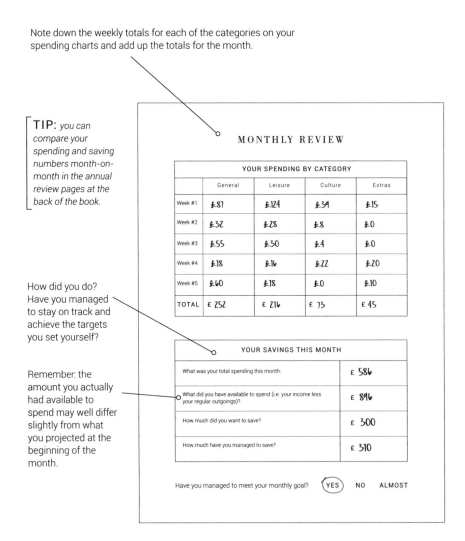

MONTHLY REVIEW

YOUR SPENDING BY CATEGORY

	General	Leisure	Culture	Extras
Week #1	£87	£124	£34	£15
Week #2	£32	£28	£8	£0
Week #3	£55	£30	£4	£0
Week #4	£18	£16	£22	£20
Week #5	£60	£18	£0	£10
TOTAL	£ 252	£ 216	£ 73	£ 45

YOUR SAVINGS THIS MONTH

What was your total spending this month:	£ 586
What did you have available to spend (i.e. your income less your regular outgoings)?	£ 896
How much did you want to save?	£ 300
How much have you managed to save?	£ 310

Have you managed to meet your monthly goal?　(YES)　NO　ALMOST

MONTH: __February__

Use the space below to reflect upon your successes, efforts, failures...

I just managed my savings goal, though I could have probably done without one or two trips to the pub over the month. It was a bit of a slog making lunches, but the food was a lot more interesting – no more soggy take-away sandwiches for me!

TIP: *reflecting on your aims will give you a springboard for the next month.*

"Awareness is the greatest agent for change."
ECKHART TOLLE

TO SAVE OR TO SPEND?

Are you considering buying something but aren't sure whether or not to go ahead?
This flow chart will help you to decide if it's a wise choice, or if it would be better to put
this money in the piggybank, or even spend it on something more useful...

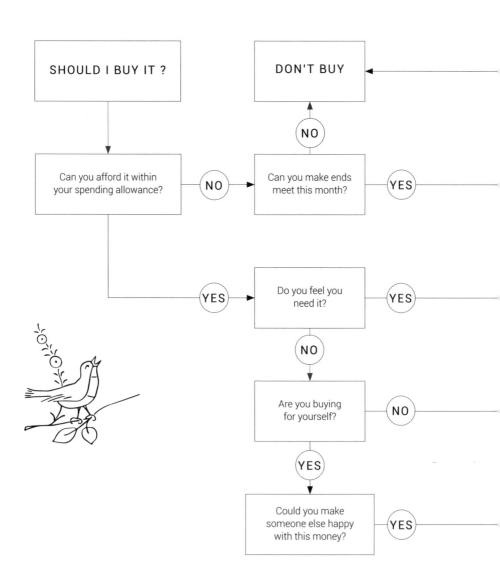

SHOULD I BUY IT ?

DON'T BUY

Can you afford it within your spending allowance?

NO

Can you make ends meet this month?

NO

YES

YES

Do you feel you need it?

YES

NO

Are you buying for yourself?

NO

YES

Could you make someone else happy with this money?

YES

"No snowflake ever falls in the wrong place."
ZEN PROVERB

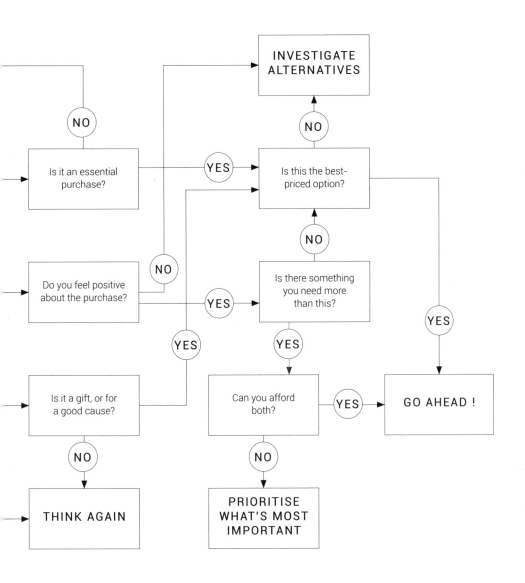

ANTICIPATE THE UNFORESEEN

Use these tables to jot down any one-off expenses that are likely to crop up through the year, such as birthday presents, family events, travel, etc...

JANUARY		FEBRUARY		MARCH	
Item	Amount	Item	Amount	Item	Amount

APRIL		MAY		JUNE	
Item	Amount	Item	Amount	Item	Amount

Although you will record these sorts of expenses as 'Unexpected Extras' in the Weekly Diary, it's best to anticipate them so you know when they are coming and can adapt your budget accordingly.

JULY		AUGUST		SEPTEMBER	
Item	Amount	Item	Amount	Item	Amount

OCTOBER		NOVEMBER		DECEMBER	
Item	Amount	Item	Amount	Item	Amount

THE YEAR BEGINS

PLANNING THE MONTH AHEAD

Note down your projected income for the month:

INCOME *(e.g. salary, freelance work, benefits, lodger...)*		
Date	Source	Amount
	TOTAL	£

And list your regular expenses and outgoings:

REGULAR OUTGOINGS *(e.g. rent/mortgage, utilities, phone, parking permit, gym membership, home/car/health insurance, credit cards/loans...)*			
Bill / expense	Amount	Bill / expense	Amount
		TOTAL	£

MONTH: ....

Work out how much you have to spend this month and
decide what you want to save:

Total projected income:	£
Less regular expenses:	£
What's left for you to spend?	£
How much do you want to save this month?	£

What are your aims for this month?

....

....

....

And how do you hope to achieve them?

....

....

....

WEEKLY SPENDING

	Monday	Tuesday	Wednesday	Thursday ....
General				
Leisure				
Culture				
Unexpected Extras				

MONTH: ....

	Friday	Saturday	Sunday	**TOTAL**
General				
Leisure				
Culture				
Unexpected Extras				

WEEKLY SPENDING

	Monday	Tuesday	Wednesday	Thursday ....
General				
Leisure				
Culture				
Unexpected Extras				

MONTH: ....

	Friday	Saturday	Sunday	TOTAL
General				
Leisure				
Culture				
Unexpected Extras				

WEEKLY SPENDING

	Monday	Tuesday	Wednesday	Thursday ....
General				
Leisure				
Culture				
Unexpected Extras				

MONTH: ....

	Friday	Saturday	Sunday	TOTAL
General				
Leisure				
Culture				
Unexpected Extras				

WEEKLY SPENDING

	Monday	Tuesday	Wednesday	Thursday ....
General				
Leisure				
Culture				
Unexpected Extras				

MONTH: ....

	Friday	Saturday	Sunday	TOTAL
General				
Leisure				
Culture				
Unexpected Extras				

WEEKLY SPENDING

	Monday	Tuesday	Wednesday	Thursday ....
General				
Leisure				
Culture				
Unexpected Extras				

MONTH: ....

	Friday	Saturday	Sunday	TOTAL
General				
Leisure				
Culture				
Unexpected Extras				

MONTHLY REVIEW

YOUR SPENDING BY CATEGORY				
	General	Leisure	Culture	Extras
Week #1				
Week #2				
Week #3				
Week #4				
Week #5				
TOTAL	£	£	£	£

YOUR SAVINGS THIS MONTH	
What was your total spending this month:	£
What did you have available to spend (i.e. your income less your regular outgoings)?	£
How much did you want to save?	£
How much have you managed to save?	£

Have you managed to meet your monthly goal?   YES   NO   ALMOST

MONTH: ....

Use the space below to reflect upon your successes, efforts, failures...

"As a bee gathering nectar does not harm or
disturb the colour and fragrance of the flower,
so do the wise move through the world."

BUDDHA

PLANNING THE MONTH AHEAD

Note down your projected income for the month:

INCOME (e.g. salary, freelance work, benefits, lodger...)		
Date	Source	Amount
	TOTAL	£

And list your regular expenses and outgoings:

REGULAR OUTGOINGS (e.g. rent/mortgage, utilities, phone, parking permit, gym membership, home/car/health insurance, credit cards/loans...)			
Bill / expense	Amount	Bill / expense	Amount
		TOTAL	£

MONTH: ....

Work out how much you have to spend this month and
decide what you want to save:

Total projected income:	£
Less regular expenses:	£
What's left for you to spend?	£
How much do you want to save this month?	£

What are your aims for this month?

....

....

....

....

And how do you hope to achieve them?

....

....

....

....

WEEKLY SPENDING

	Monday	Tuesday	Wednesday	Thursday ....
General				
Leisure				
Culture				
Unexpected Extras				

MONTH: ....

	Friday	Saturday	Sunday	TOTAL
General				
Leisure				
Culture				
Unexpected Extras				

WEEKLY SPENDING

	Monday	Tuesday	Wednesday	Thursday ....
General				
Leisure				
Culture				
Unexpected Extras				

MONTH: ....

	Friday	Saturday	Sunday	TOTAL
General				
Leisure				
Culture				
Unexpected Extras				

WEEKLY SPENDING

	Monday	Tuesday	Wednesday	Thursday ....
General				
Leisure				
Culture				
Unexpected Extras				

MONTH: ....

	Friday	Saturday	Sunday	TOTAL
General				
Leisure				
Culture				
Unexpected Extras				

WEEKLY SPENDING

	Monday	Tuesday	Wednesday	Thursday ....
General				
Leisure				
Culture				
Unexpected Extras				

MONTH: ....

	Friday	Saturday	Sunday	TOTAL
General				
Leisure				
Culture				
Unexpected Extras				

WEEKLY SPENDING

	Monday	Tuesday	Wednesday	Thursday ....
General				
Leisure				
Culture				
Unexpected Extras				

MONTH: ....

	Friday	Saturday	Sunday	TOTAL
General				
Leisure				
Culture				
Unexpected Extras				

MONTHLY REVIEW

YOUR SPENDING BY CATEGORY				
	General	Leisure	Culture	Extras
Week #1				
Week #2				
Week #3				
Week #4				
Week #5				
TOTAL	£	£	£	£

YOUR SAVINGS THIS MONTH	
What was your total spending this month:	£
What did you have available to spend (i.e. your income less your regular outgoings)?	£
How much did you want to save?	£
How much have you managed to save?	£

Have you managed to meet your monthly goal?   YES   NO   ALMOST

MONTH: ....

Use the space below to reflect upon your successes, efforts, failures...

....

....

....

....

....

....

....

DECLUTTER

Clear out anything in your home that you don't
need but haven't yet got round to throwing away.
Keep only the things you really love. The Japanese
believe that tidiness of the space around you
translates into internal order and calm.

PLANNING THE MONTH AHEAD

Note down your projected income for the month:

INCOME *(e.g. salary, freelance work, benefits, lodger...)*		
Date	Source	Amount
	TOTAL	£

And list your regular expenses and outgoings:

REGULAR OUTGOINGS *(e.g. rent/mortgage, utilities, phone, parking permit, gym membership, home/car/health insurance, credit cards/loans...)*

Bill / expense	Amount	Bill / expense	Amount
		TOTAL	£

MONTH: ....

Work out how much you have to spend this month and
decide what you want to save:

Total projected income:	£
Less regular expenses:	£
What's left for you to spend?	£
How much do you want to save this month?	£

What are your aims for this month?

....

....

....

....

And how do you hope to achieve them?

....

....

....

....

WEEKLY SPENDING

	Monday	Tuesday	Wednesday	Thursday ....
General				
Leisure				
Culture				
Unexpected Extras				

MONTH: ....

	Friday	Saturday	Sunday	TOTAL
General				
Leisure				
Culture				
Unexpected Extras				

WEEKLY SPENDING

	Monday	Tuesday	Wednesday	Thursday ....
General				
Leisure				
Culture				
Unexpected Extras				

MONTH: ....

	Friday	Saturday	Sunday	TOTAL
General				
Leisure				
Culture				
Unexpected Extras				

WEEKLY SPENDING

	Monday	Tuesday	Wednesday	Thursday ....
General				
Leisure				
Culture				
Unexpected Extras				

MONTH: ....

	Friday	Saturday	Sunday	TOTAL
General				
Leisure				
Culture				
Unexpected Extras				

WEEKLY SPENDING

	Monday	Tuesday	Wednesday	Thursday ....
General				
Leisure				
Culture				
Unexpected Extras				

MONTH: ....

	Friday	Saturday	Sunday	**TOTAL**
General				
Leisure				
Culture				
Unexpected Extras				

WEEKLY SPENDING

	Monday	Tuesday	Wednesday	Thursday ....
General				
Leisure				
Culture				
Unexpected Extras				

MONTH: ....

	Friday	Saturday	Sunday	TOTAL
General				
Leisure				
Culture				
Unexpected Extras				

MONTHLY REVIEW

YOUR SPENDING BY CATEGORY				
	General	Leisure	Culture	Extras
Week #1				
Week #2				
Week #3				
Week #4				
Week #5				
TOTAL	£	£	£	£

YOUR SAVINGS THIS MONTH	
What was your total spending this month:	£
What did you have available to spend (i.e. your income less your regular outgoings)?	£
How much did you want to save?	£
How much have you managed to save?	£

Have you managed to meet your monthly goal?   YES   NO   ALMOST

MONTH: ....

Use the space below to reflect upon your successes, efforts, failures...

"Have good trust in yourself... not in the
One that you think you should be, but in
the One that you are."

MAEZUMI ROSHI

PLANNING THE MONTH AHEAD

Note down your projected income for the month:

INCOME (e.g. salary, freelance work, benefits, lodger...)		
Date	Source	Amount
	TOTAL	£

And list your regular expenses and outgoings:

REGULAR OUTGOINGS (e.g. rent/mortgage, utilities, phone, parking permit, gym membership, home/car/health insurance, credit cards/loans...)

Bill / expense	Amount	Bill / expense	Amount
		TOTAL	£

MONTH: ....

Work out how much you have to spend this month and
decide what you want to save:

Total projected income:	£
Less regular expenses:	£
What's left for you to spend?	£
How much do you want to save this month?	£

What are your aims for this month?

....

....

....

....

And how do you hope to achieve them?

....

....

....

....

WEEKLY SPENDING

	Monday	Tuesday	Wednesday	Thursday ....
General				
Leisure				
Culture				
Unexpected Extras				

MONTH: ....

	Friday	Saturday	Sunday	TOTAL
General				
Leisure				
Culture				
Unexpected Extras				

WEEKLY SPENDING

	Monday	Tuesday	Wednesday	Thursday ....
General				
Leisure				
Culture				
Unexpected Extras				

MONTH: ....

	Friday	Saturday	Sunday	TOTAL
General				
Leisure				
Culture				
Unexpected Extras				

WEEKLY SPENDING

	Monday	Tuesday	Wednesday	Thursday ....
General				
Leisure				
Culture				
Unexpected Extras				

MONTH: ....

	Friday	Saturday	Sunday	TOTAL
General				
Leisure				
Culture				
Unexpected Extras				

WEEKLY SPENDING

	Monday	Tuesday	Wednesday	Thursday ....
General				
Leisure				
Culture				
Unexpected Extras				

MONTH: ....

	Friday	Saturday	Sunday	TOTAL
General				
Leisure				
Culture				
Unexpected Extras				

WEEKLY SPENDING

	Monday	Tuesday	Wednesday	Thursday ....
General				
Leisure				
Culture				
Unexpected Extras				

MONTH: ....

	Friday	Saturday	Sunday	TOTAL
General				
Leisure				
Culture				
Unexpected Extras				

MONTHLY REVIEW

YOUR SPENDING BY CATEGORY				
	General	Leisure	Culture	Extras
Week #1				
Week #2				
Week #3				
Week #4				
Week #5				
TOTAL	£	£	£	£

YOUR SAVINGS THIS MONTH	
What was your total spending this month:	£
What did you have available to spend (i.e. your income less your regular outgoings)?	£
How much did you want to save?	£
How much have you managed to save?	£

Have you managed to meet your monthly goal?   YES   NO   ALMOST

MONTH: ....

Use the space below to reflect upon your successes, efforts, failures...

....

....

....

....

....

....

"The way to wealth is as plain as the
way to market... waste neither time nor
money, but make the best use of both."

BENJAMIN FRANKLIN

PLANNING THE MONTH AHEAD

Note down your projected income for the month:

INCOME *(e.g. salary, freelance work, benefits, lodger...)*		
Date	Source	Amount
	TOTAL	£

And list your regular expenses and outgoings:

REGULAR OUTGOINGS *(e.g. rent/mortgage, utilities, phone, parking permit, gym membership, home/car/health insurance, credit cards/loans...)*			
Bill / expense	Amount	Bill / expense	Amount
		TOTAL	£

MONTH:

Work out how much you have to spend this month and
decide what you want to save:

Total projected income:	£
Less regular expenses:	£
What's left for you to spend?	£
How much do you want to save this month?	£

What are your aims for this month?

....

....

....

....

And how do you hope to achieve them?

....

....

....

....

WEEKLY SPENDING

	Monday	Tuesday	Wednesday	Thursday ....
General				
Leisure				
Culture				
Unexpected Extras				

MONTH: ....

	Friday	Saturday	Sunday	TOTAL
General				
Leisure				
Culture				
Unexpected Extras				

WEEKLY SPENDING

	Monday	Tuesday	Wednesday	Thursday ....
General				
Leisure				
Culture				
Unexpected Extras				

MONTH: ....

	Friday	Saturday	Sunday	TOTAL
General				
Leisure				
Culture				
Unexpected Extras				

WEEKLY SPENDING

	Monday	Tuesday	Wednesday	Thursday ....
General				
Leisure				
Culture				
Unexpected Extras				

MONTH: ....

	Friday	Saturday	Sunday	TOTAL
General				
Leisure				
Culture				
Unexpected Extras				

WEEKLY SPENDING

	Monday	Tuesday	Wednesday	Thursday ....
General				
Leisure				
Culture				
Unexpected Extras				

MONTH: ....

	Friday	Saturday	Sunday	TOTAL
General				
Leisure				
Culture				
Unexpected Extras				

WEEKLY SPENDING

	Monday	Tuesday	Wednesday	Thursday ....
General				
Leisure				
Culture				
Unexpected Extras				

MONTH: ....

	Friday	Saturday	Sunday	TOTAL
General				
Leisure				
Culture				
Unexpected Extras				

MONTHLY REVIEW

YOUR SPENDING BY CATEGORY			
	General	Leisure	Culture	Extras
Week #1				
Week #2				
Week #3				
Week #4				
Week #5				
TOTAL	£	£	£	£

YOUR SAVINGS THIS MONTH	
What was your total spending this month:	£
What did you have available to spend (i.e. your income less your regular outgoings)?	£
How much did you want to save?	£
How much have you managed to save?	£

Have you managed to meet your monthly goal?   YES   NO   ALMOST

MONTH: ....

Use the space below to reflect upon your successes, efforts, failures...

....

....

....

....

....

....

THE POWER OF HABIT

So much of what we do every day is
performed without a moment's thought. But
you are a rational being. You have the power
to choose - to overcome the cognitive bias
that is a barrier to change. Pick one small
thing you always do, and do it differently.

PLANNING THE MONTH AHEAD

Note down your projected income for the month:

INCOME *(e.g. salary, freelance work, benefits, lodger...)*		
Date	Source	Amount
	TOTAL	£

And list your regular expenses and outgoings:

REGULAR OUTGOINGS *(e.g. rent/mortgage, utilities, phone, parking permit, gym membership, home/car/health insurance, credit cards/loans...)*			
Bill / expense	Amount	Bill / expense	Amount
		TOTAL	£

MONTH: ....

Work out how much you have to spend this month and
decide what you want to save:

Total projected income:	£
Less regular expenses:	£
What's left for you to spend?	£
How much do you want to save this month?	£

What are your aims for this month?

....

....

....

....

And how do you hope to achieve them?

....

....

....

....

WEEKLY SPENDING

	Monday	Tuesday	Wednesday	Thursday ....
General				
Leisure				
Culture				
Unexpected Extras				

MONTH: ....

	Friday	Saturday	Sunday	TOTAL
General				
Leisure				
Culture				
Unexpected Extras				

WEEKLY SPENDING

	Monday	Tuesday	Wednesday	Thursday ....
General				
Leisure				
Culture				
Unexpected Extras				

MONTH: ....

	Friday	Saturday	Sunday	TOTAL
General				
Leisure				
Culture				
Unexpected Extras				

WEEKLY SPENDING

	Monday	Tuesday	Wednesday	Thursday ....
General				
Leisure				
Culture				
Unexpected Extras				

MONTH: ....

	Friday	Saturday	Sunday	TOTAL
General				
Leisure				
Culture				
Unexpected Extras				

WEEKLY SPENDING

	Monday	Tuesday	Wednesday	Thursday ....
General				
Leisure				
Culture				
Unexpected Extras				

MONTH: ....

	Friday	Saturday	Sunday	TOTAL
General				
Leisure				
Culture				
Unexpected Extras				

WEEKLY SPENDING

	Monday	Tuesday	Wednesday	Thursday ....
General				
Leisure				
Culture				
Unexpected Extras				

MONTH: ....

	Friday	Saturday	Sunday	TOTAL
General				
Leisure				
Culture				
Unexpected Extras				

MONTHLY REVIEW

YOUR SPENDING BY CATEGORY				
	General	Leisure	Culture	Extras
Week #1				
Week #2				
Week #3				
Week #4				
Week #5				
TOTAL	£	£	£	£

YOUR SAVINGS THIS MONTH	
What was your total spending this month:	£
What did you have available to spend (i.e. your income less your regular outgoings)?	£
How much did you want to save?	£
How much have you managed to save?	£

Have you managed to meet your monthly goal?   **YES**   **NO**   **ALMOST**

MONTH:

Use the space below to reflect upon your successes, efforts, failures...

"Drink your tea slowly and reverently, as if it
is the axis on which the world earth revolves -
slowly, evenly, without rushing toward the future."

THICH NHAT HANH

PLANNING THE MONTH AHEAD

Note down your projected income for the month:

INCOME *(e.g. salary, freelance work, benefits, lodger...)*		
Date	Source	Amount
	TOTAL	£

And list your regular expenses and outgoings:

REGULAR OUTGOINGS *(e.g. rent/mortgage, utilities, phone, parking permit, gym membership, home/car/health insurance, credit cards/loans...)*			
Bill / expense	Amount	Bill / expense	Amount
		TOTAL	£

MONTH:

Work out how much you have to spend this month and
decide what you want to save:

Total projected income:	£
Less regular expenses:	£
What's left for you to spend?	£
How much do you want to save this month?	£

What are your aims for this month?

....

....

....

....

And how do you hope to achieve them?

....

....

....

....

WEEKLY SPENDING

	Monday	Tuesday	Wednesday	Thursday ....
General				
Leisure				
Culture				
Unexpected Extras				

MONTH: ....

	Friday	Saturday	Sunday	TOTAL
General				
Leisure				
Culture				
Unexpected Extras				

WEEKLY SPENDING

	Monday	Tuesday	Wednesday	Thursday ....
General				
Leisure				
Culture				
Unexpected Extras				

MONTH: ....

	Friday	Saturday	Sunday	TOTAL
General				
Leisure				
Culture				
Unexpected Extras				

WEEKLY SPENDING

	Monday	Tuesday	Wednesday	Thursday ....
General				
Leisure				
Culture				
Unexpected Extras				

MONTH: ....

	Friday	Saturday	Sunday	TOTAL
General				
Leisure				
Culture				
Unexpected Extras				

WEEKLY SPENDING

	Monday	Tuesday	Wednesday	Thursday ....
General				
Leisure				
Culture				
Unexpected Extras				

MONTH: ....

	Friday	Saturday	Sunday	TOTAL
General				
Leisure				
Culture				
Unexpected Extras				

WEEKLY SPENDING

	Monday	Tuesday	Wednesday	Thursday ....
General				
Leisure				
Culture				
Unexpected Extras				

MONTH: ....

	Friday	Saturday	Sunday	TOTAL
General				
Leisure				
Culture				
Unexpected Extras				

MONTHLY REVIEW

YOUR SPENDING BY CATEGORY				
	General	Leisure	Culture	Extras
Week #1				
Week #2				
Week #3				
Week #4				
Week #5				
TOTAL	£	£	£	£

YOUR SAVINGS THIS MONTH	
What was your total spending this month:	£
What did you have available to spend (i.e. your income less your regular outgoings)?	£
How much did you want to save?	£
How much have you managed to save?	£

Have you managed to meet your monthly goal?   YES   NO   ALMOST

MONTH:

Use the space below to reflect upon your successes, efforts, failures...

INVEST WISELY

The Japanese art of saving money is about the
sustained sense of wellbeing that comes from
being on top of your finances, along with other
aspects of your life. Wherever possible try to
buy well. Get something that will last: this will
be more fulfilling in the long run.

PLANNING THE MONTH AHEAD

Note down your projected income for the month:

INCOME *(e.g. salary, freelance work, benefits, lodger...)*		
Date	Source	Amount
	TOTAL	£

And list your regular expenses and outgoings:

REGULAR OUTGOINGS *(e.g. rent/mortgage, utilities, phone, parking permit, gym membership, home/car/health insurance, credit cards/loans...)*			
Bill / expense	Amount	Bill / expense	Amount
		TOTAL	£

MONTH:

Work out how much you have to spend this month and
decide what you want to save:

Total projected income:	£
Less regular expenses:	£
What's left for you to spend?	£
How much do you want to save this month?	£

What are your aims for this month?

....

....

....

....

And how do you hope to achieve them?

....

....

....

....

WEEKLY SPENDING

	Monday ………	Tuesday ………	Wednesday ………	Thursday ………
General				
Leisure				
Culture				
Unexpected Extras				

MONTH: ....

	Friday	Saturday	Sunday	**TOTAL**
General				
Leisure				
Culture				
Unexpected Extras				

WEEKLY SPENDING

	Monday	Tuesday	Wednesday	Thursday ....
General				
Leisure				
Culture				
Unexpected Extras				

MONTH: ....

	Friday	Saturday	Sunday	TOTAL
General				
Leisure				
Culture				
Unexpected Extras				

WEEKLY SPENDING

	Monday	Tuesday	Wednesday	Thursday ....
General				
Leisure				
Culture				
Unexpected Extras				

MONTH: ....

	Friday	Saturday	Sunday	TOTAL
General				
Leisure				
Culture				
Unexpected Extras				

WEEKLY SPENDING

	Monday	Tuesday	Wednesday	Thursday ....
General				
Leisure				
Culture				
Unexpected Extras				

MONTH: ....

	Friday	Saturday	Sunday	TOTAL
General				
Leisure				
Culture				
Unexpected Extras				

WEEKLY SPENDING

	Monday	Tuesday	Wednesday	Thursday ....
General				
Leisure				
Culture				
Unexpected Extras				

MONTH: ....

	Friday	Saturday	Sunday	TOTAL
General				
Leisure				
Culture				
Unexpected Extras				

MONTHLY REVIEW

YOUR SPENDING BY CATEGORY				
	General	Leisure	Culture	Extras
Week #1				
Week #2				
Week #3				
Week #4				
Week #5				
TOTAL	£	£	£	£

YOUR SAVINGS THIS MONTH	
What was your total spending this month:	£
What did you have available to spend (i.e. your income less your regular outgoings)?	£
How much did you want to save?	£
How much have you managed to save?	£

Have you managed to meet your monthly goal?   YES   NO   ALMOST

MONTH:

Use the space below to reflect upon your successes, efforts, failures...

"A journey of a thousand miles begins
with a single step."

LAO TZU

PLANNING THE MONTH AHEAD

Note down your projected income for the month:

INCOME *(e.g. salary, freelance work, benefits, lodger...)*		
Date	Source	Amount
	TOTAL	£

And list your regular expenses and outgoings:

REGULAR OUTGOINGS *(e.g. rent/mortgage, utilities, phone, parking permit, gym membership, home/car/health insurance, credit cards/loans...)*			
Bill / expense	Amount	Bill / expense	Amount
		TOTAL	£

MONTH:
....

Work out how much you have to spend this month and
decide what you want to save:

Total projected income:	£
Less regular expenses:	£
What's left for you to spend?	£
How much do you want to save this month?	£

What are your aims for this month?

....

....

....

....

And how do you hope to achieve them?

....

....

....

....

WEEKLY SPENDING

	Monday	Tuesday	Wednesday	Thursday ....
General				
Leisure				
Culture				
Unexpected Extras				

MONTH: ....

	Friday	Saturday	Sunday	TOTAL
General				
Leisure				
Culture				
Unexpected Extras				

WEEKLY SPENDING

	Monday	Tuesday	Wednesday	Thursday ....
General				
Leisure				
Culture				
Unexpected Extras				

MONTH: ....

	Friday	Saturday	Sunday	TOTAL
General				
Leisure				
Culture				
Unexpected Extras				

WEEKLY SPENDING

	Monday	Tuesday	Wednesday	Thursday ....
General				
Leisure				
Culture				
Unexpected Extras				

MONTH: ....

	Friday	Saturday	Sunday	TOTAL
General				
Leisure				
Culture				
Unexpected Extras				

WEEKLY SPENDING

	Monday	Tuesday	Wednesday	Thursday ....
General				
Leisure				
Culture				
Unexpected Extras				

MONTH: _____

	Friday	Saturday	Sunday	TOTAL
General				
Leisure				
Culture				
Unexpected Extras				

WEEKLY SPENDING

	Monday	Tuesday	Wednesday	Thursday ....
General				
Leisure				
Culture				
Unexpected Extras				

MONTH: ....

	Friday	Saturday	Sunday	TOTAL
General				
Leisure				
Culture				
Unexpected Extras				

MONTHLY REVIEW

YOUR SPENDING BY CATEGORY				
	General	Leisure	Culture	Extras
Week #1				
Week #2				
Week #3				
Week #4				
Week #5				
TOTAL	£	£	£	£

YOUR SAVINGS THIS MONTH	
What was your total spending this month:	£
What did you have available to spend (i.e. your income less your regular outgoings)?	£
How much did you want to save?	£
How much have you managed to save?	£

Have you managed to meet your monthly goal?   YES   NO   ALMOST

MONTH: ....

Use the space below to reflect upon your successes, efforts, failures...

"The art of living is neither careless drifting on the
one hand nor fearful clinging to the past on the
other. It consists in being sensitive to each moment,
in regarding it as utterly new and unique, in
having the mind open and wholly receptive."

ALAN WATTS

PLANNING THE MONTH AHEAD

Note down your projected income for the month:

INCOME *(e.g. salary, freelance work, benefits, lodger...)*		
Date	Source	Amount
	TOTAL	£

And list your regular expenses and outgoings:

REGULAR OUTGOINGS *(e.g. rent/mortgage, utilities, phone, parking permit, gym membership, home/car/health insurance, credit cards/loans...)*			
Bill / expense	Amount	Bill / expense	Amount
		TOTAL	£

MONTH:

Work out how much you have to spend this month and
decide what you want to save:

Total projected income:	£
Less regular expenses:	£
What's left for you to spend?	£
How much do you want to save this month?	£

What are your aims for this month?

And how do you hope to achieve them?

WEEKLY SPENDING

	Monday	Tuesday	Wednesday	Thursday ....
General				
Leisure				
Culture				
Unexpected Extras				

MONTH: ....

	Friday	Saturday	Sunday	TOTAL
General				
Leisure				
Culture				
Unexpected Extras				

WEEKLY SPENDING

	Monday	Tuesday	Wednesday	Thursday ....
General				
Leisure				
Culture				
Unexpected Extras				

MONTH: ....

	Friday	Saturday	Sunday	TOTAL
General				
Leisure				
Culture				
Unexpected Extras				

WEEKLY SPENDING

	Monday	Tuesday	Wednesday	Thursday ....
General				
Leisure				
Culture				
Unexpected Extras				

MONTH: ....

	Friday	Saturday	Sunday	TOTAL
General				
Leisure				
Culture				
Unexpected Extras				

WEEKLY SPENDING

·	Monday	Tuesday	Wednesday	Thursday ....
General				
Leisure				
Culture				
Unexpected Extras				

MONTH: ....

	Friday	Saturday	Sunday	TOTAL
General				
Leisure				
Culture				
Unexpected Extras				

WEEKLY SPENDING

	Monday	Tuesday	Wednesday	Thursday ....
General				
Leisure				
Culture				
Unexpected Extras				

MONTH: ....

	Friday	Saturday	Sunday	TOTAL
General				
Leisure				
Culture				
Unexpected Extras				

MONTHLY REVIEW

YOUR SPENDING BY CATEGORY				
	General	Leisure	Culture	Extras
Week #1				
Week #2				
Week #3				
Week #4				
Week #5				
TOTAL	£	£	£	£

YOUR SAVINGS THIS MONTH	
What was your total spending this month:	£
What did you have available to spend (i.e. your income less your regular outgoings)?	£
How much did you want to save?	£
How much have you managed to save?	£

Have you managed to meet your monthly goal?   YES   NO   ALMOST

MONTH: ....

Use the space below to reflect upon your successes, efforts, failures...

....

....

....

....

....

....

....

"Before enlightenment; chop wood, carry water.
After enlightenment; chop wood, carry water."
BUDDHA

PLANNING THE MONTH AHEAD

Note down your projected income for the month:

INCOME *(e.g. salary, freelance work, benefits, lodger...)*		
Date	Source	Amount
	TOTAL	£

And list your regular expenses and outgoings:

REGULAR OUTGOINGS *(e.g. rent/mortgage, utilities, phone, parking permit, gym membership, home/car/health insurance, credit cards/loans...)*			
Bill / expense	Amount	Bill / expense	Amount
		TOTAL	£

MONTH:

Work out how much you have to spend this month and
decide what you want to save:

Total projected income:	£
Less regular expenses:	£
What's left for you to spend?	£
How much do you want to save this month?	£

What are your aims for this month?

....

....

....

....

And how do you hope to achieve them?

....

....

....

....

WEEKLY SPENDING

	Monday	Tuesday	Wednesday	Thursday ....
General				
Leisure				
Culture				
Unexpected Extras				

MONTH: ....

	Friday	Saturday	Sunday	TOTAL
General				
Leisure				
Culture				
Unexpected Extras				

WEEKLY SPENDING

	Monday	Tuesday	Wednesday	Thursday ....
General				
Leisure				
Culture				
Unexpected Extras				

MONTH: ....

	Friday	Saturday	Sunday	TOTAL
General				
Leisure				
Culture				
Unexpected Extras				

WEEKLY SPENDING

	Monday	Tuesday	Wednesday	Thursday ....
General				
Leisure				
Culture				
Unexpected Extras				

MONTH: _____

	Friday	Saturday	Sunday	TOTAL
General				
Leisure				
Culture				
Unexpected Extras				

WEEKLY SPENDING

	Monday	Tuesday	Wednesday	Thursday ....
General				
Leisure				
Culture				
Unexpected Extras				

MONTH: ....

	Friday	Saturday	Sunday	**TOTAL**
General				
Leisure				
Culture				
Unexpected Extras				

WEEKLY SPENDING

	Monday	Tuesday	Wednesday	Thursday ....
General				
Leisure				
Culture				
Unexpected Extras				

MONTH: ....

	Friday	Saturday	Sunday	TOTAL
General				
Leisure				
Culture				
Unexpected Extras				

MONTHLY REVIEW

YOUR SPENDING BY CATEGORY				
	General	Leisure	Culture	Extras
Week #1				
Week #2				
Week #3				
Week #4				
Week #5				
TOTAL	£	£	£	£

YOUR SAVINGS THIS MONTH	
What was your total spending this month:	£
What did you have available to spend (i.e. your income less your regular outgoings)?	£
How much did you want to save?	£
How much have you managed to save?	£

Have you managed to meet your monthly goal?   YES   NO   ALMOST

MONTH: ....

Use the space below to reflect upon your successes, efforts, failures...

"Self-realisation is effortless. What you are
trying to find is what you already are."

RAMESH BALSEKAR

PLANNING THE MONTH AHEAD

Note down your projected income for the month:

INCOME *(e.g. salary, freelance work, benefits, lodger...)*		
Date	Source	Amount
	TOTAL	£

And list your regular expenses and outgoings:

REGULAR OUTGOINGS *(e.g. rent/mortgage, utilities, phone, parking permit, gym membership, home/car/health insurance, credit cards/loans...)*			
Bill / expense	Amount	Bill / expense	Amount
		TOTAL	£

MONTH:

Work out how much you have to spend this month and
decide what you want to save:

Total projected income:	£
Less regular expenses:	£
What's left for you to spend?	£
How much do you want to save this month?	£

What are your aims for this month?

....

....

....

....

And how do you hope to achieve them?

....

....

....

....

WEEKLY SPENDING

	Monday	Tuesday	Wednesday	Thursday ....
General				
Leisure				
Culture				
Unexpected Extras				

MONTH: ....

	Friday	Saturday	Sunday	TOTAL
General				
Leisure				
Culture				
Unexpected Extras				

WEEKLY SPENDING

	Monday	Tuesday	Wednesday	Thursday ....
General				
Leisure				
Culture				
Unexpected Extras				

MONTH: ....

	Friday	Saturday	Sunday	TOTAL
General				
Leisure				
Culture				
Unexpected Extras				

WEEKLY SPENDING

	Monday	Tuesday	Wednesday	Thursday ....
General				
Leisure				
Culture				
Unexpected Extras				

MONTH: ....

	Friday	Saturday	Sunday	**TOTAL**
General				
Leisure				
Culture				
Unexpected Extras				

WEEKLY SPENDING

	Monday	Tuesday	Wednesday	Thursday ....
General				
Leisure				
Culture				
Unexpected Extras				

MONTH: ....

	Friday	Saturday	Sunday	**TOTAL**
General				
Leisure				
Culture				
Unexpected Extras				

WEEKLY SPENDING

	Monday	Tuesday	Wednesday	Thursday ....
General				
Leisure				
Culture				
Unexpected Extras				

MONTH: ....

	Friday	Saturday	Sunday	**TOTAL**
General				
Leisure				
Culture				
Unexpected Extras				

MONTHLY REVIEW

YOUR SPENDING BY CATEGORY			
	General	Leisure	Culture	Extras
Week #1				
Week #2				
Week #3				
Week #4				
Week #5				
TOTAL	£	£	£	£

YOUR SAVINGS THIS MONTH	
What was your total spending this month:	£
What did you have available to spend (i.e. your income less your regular outgoings)?	£
How much did you want to save?	£
How much have you managed to save?	£

Have you managed to meet your monthly goal?   **YES   NO   ALMOST**

MONTH: ....

Use the space below to reflect upon your successes, efforts, failures...

....

....

....

....

....

....

....

"The habit of saving is itself an education.
It cultivates a sense of order, fosters
every virtue, teaches self-denial and
so broadens the mind."

T T MUNGER

ANNUAL REVIEW

YOUR ANNUAL SPENDING AT A GLANCE

Look back to your Monthly Review pages and tot up your total spending by category.

Calculate each category as a percentage of your total expenditure (divide the category figure by the total and multiply by 100).

Plot the percentages on the pie chart below to see where your money is going. The pie is divided into 100 segments to make this easy.

ANNUAL EXPENDITURE

General	£	%
Leisure	£	%
Culture	£	%
Extras	£	%
TOTAL	£	

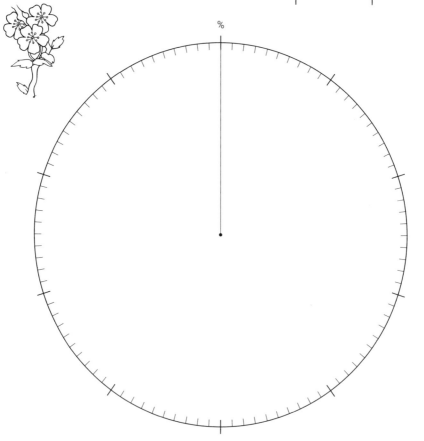

%

PLOT YOUR ANNUAL INCOME, SPENDING AND SAVINGS AS A GRAPH

Bring forward the figures from your Monthly Review pages for (i) what you had available to spend (i.e. your income less your regular outgoings), (ii) your total everyday expenditure, and (iii) what you managed to save each month.

Plot them on the graph using a different colour for each to make it easier to decipher. Where have you accumulated savings? Where is your everyday expenditure eating into your bank balance?

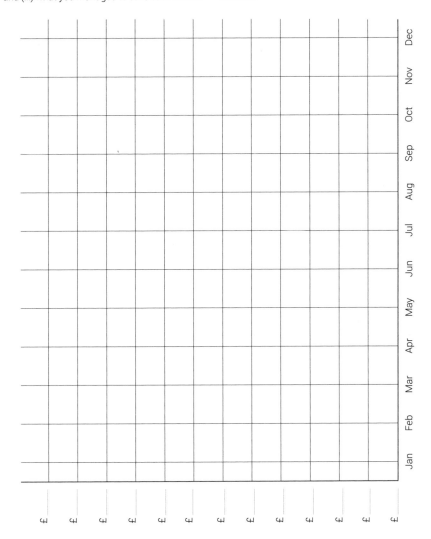

TIME TO REFLECT - QUESTIONNAIRE

Of course, it's not all about the numbers; it's important that you take time to reflect upon the last 12 months and consider the positives from the year, where you've benefitted from your approach to your finances, and where you might look to make changes going forward.

1. What new habits have you added to your life from using your Kakebo?

2. What have you given up?

3. Is there anything you have missed?

4. Did you make the changes you needed/ wanted to be able to achieve your financial and savings goals?

☐ Yes
☐ No
☐ I might have done better

Other thoughts:

5. What changes were hardest to implement and/or keep?

6. Why?

☐ My daily routine made it difficult
☐ I didn't feel fully committed
☐ Life changes got in the way
☐ I needed a more flexible approach
☐ Other / further thoughts:

7. What goals were you unable to achieve?

8. Why?

☐ I needed more time than I expected
☐ They weren't very realistic
☐ My objectives changed
☐ Other / further thoughts:

9. What will you change about your approach, habits or your goals themselves to achieve them in the next 12 months?

_____
_____
_____
_____
_____
_____
_____
_____

10. What area of your spending has surprised you the most?

☐ General expenses
☐ Leisure
☐ Culture
☐ Unexpected extras

Other thoughts about why and in what way:

_____
_____
_____
_____
_____

11. Which month was your most expensive?

☐ January   ☐ July
☐ February   ☐ August
☐ March   ☐ September
☐ April   ☐ October
☐ May   ☐ November
☐ June   ☐ December

12. Why?

☐ Unexpected expenses
☐ More leisure spending
☐ I lost track of my daily spending
☐ Gifts / events for family and friends
☐ Other / further thoughts:

_____
_____
_____
_____

13. Which month(s) felt the most positive / most under control?

☐ January   ☐ July
☐ February   ☐ August
☐ March   ☐ September
☐ April   ☐ October
☐ May   ☐ November
☐ June   ☐ December

14. Why?

☐ I easily achieved my savings goal
☐ I made positive changes to my habits
☐ I improved my spending
☐ I received extra income
☐ Other / further thoughts:

_____
_____
_____
_____
_____

15. Regarding spending and saving, do you feel any of the below apply more than they used to?

☐ Money is a means, not an end
☐ I am more aware of the implications of my spending habits
☐ I am in control of my finances

Other thoughts:

_____
_____
_____
_____

16. What has made you happiest this year?

_____
_____
_____
_____

Published in the UK in 2017 by Short Books
Unit 316, ScreenWorks,
22 Highbury Grove,
London N5 2ER

10 9 8 7 6 5 4 3

Kakebo © 2015

Original idea by Blackie Books S.L.U.
Original Spanish language text:
Raúl Sánchez Serrano

English edition: Short Books Ltd
The English edition is published by
arrangement with Blackie Books S.L.U.
c/o MB Agencia Literaria S.L.

A CIP catalogue record for this book is available from
the British Library.

ISBN 978-1-78072-343-3

Printed and bound in Italy by L.E.G.O. Group SpA

Design by Georgia Vaux